# WORDS EVERY **PROFESSIONAL** SHOULD KNOW

Helping Professionals Talk the Talk

BY: Shanley D. McCray

Copyright © 2015 Opportune Independent Publishing Company

All rights reserved. No part of this publication may be reproduced, distributed, or transmitted in any form or by any means, including photocopying, recording, or other electronic or mechanical methods, without the prior written permission of the publisher, except in the case of brief quotations embodied in critical reviews and certain other noncommercial uses permitted by copyright law.

ISBN-10: 09965694-8-0
ISBN-13: 978-0-9965694-8-4

Printed in the United States of America.

For permission requests, write to the publisher, addressed "Attention: Permissions Coordinator," at the address below.

info@opportunepublishing.com
www.opportunepublishing.com

## Disclaimer

Although the author and publisher have made every effort to ensure that the information in this book was correct at press time, the author and publisher do not assume and hereby disclaim any liability to any party for any loss, damage, or disruption caused by errors or omissions, whether such errors or omissions result from negligence, accident, or any other cause.

# Table of contents

| | |
|---|---|
| **Preface** | 7 |
| **How to Use** | 11 |
| **General Professionals** | 13 |
| **Business** | 29 |
| **Communications** | 49 |
| **Finance** | 46 |
| **Health & Wellness** | 51 |
| **Transportation** | 56 |

# PREFACE

Before starting any job it is 100% natural to be nervous. But the reason you are nervous can tell more stories than one. Maybe you're switching careers and are unsure about whether it was a good decision, or not. Or, you just graduated from college, with no work experience, and fear the past few years didn't 100% prepare you for this role. On the other hand, you have been working for years and just received a promotion. The only issue is that you do not have much experience in your new role and fear the unknown.

If any of these scenarios fit you, or are similar to your situation, there are only a few things you can do in order to turn nervousness into confidence. In order to not turn this opportunity down and go back to your comfort zone, you can learn to talk the talk and it will began to fit comfortably as if it were tailored to you exactly.

As professionals, you must learn the words that are commonly used in order to speak the language within your respective industry. This book offers a vast compilation of words that all professionals should include within their vocabulary to sound more conversant and professional.

For instance, when we are speaking more loosely we would typically describe some words as slang. But instead the more refined way to characterize these words is jargon. Which even has another level because certain industries have a language that is of its own, which could be termed jargon as well.

Another example is in the professional world minutes take on another meaning as well. When you are having a meeting, someone may ask that minutes be recorded. If this is your first time hearing this, you may think how can this be done? By recording the clock? Well, no. It actually means taking notes of what is discussed during the meeting. Although very simple, this is a business environment term that can be easily confused.

These are very basic examples. But to someone who has never been in a specific industry or has yet to work as a professional, it is easy to become lost in translation or sound inexperienced. So in order to sound the part in which you will become, you can start here. You now have access to professional lingo, which will help you keep up in conversation, translate emails and assist with improving your business communications all around.

*Words Every Professional Should Know: Helping Professionals Talk the Talk* is for all professionals in all industries. It doesn't matter your specific title, level or industry, these words will help you sound more professional in everyday conversation, be it oral or written.

There are additional sections for words that may be more relevant and prevalent within certain industries, but are not limited to them. Every word within this book is great to know as a new, or more adept, professional.

Words Every Professional Should Know

# HOW TO USE

As a professional, you had to go through some sense of training or learning in order to be in the position that you are. During that time, or prior to, you had to know or realize how you learned in order to retain the information. Being that there are several different techniques, it is important to tap into the one that works best for you in order to increase your vocabulary over a period of time.

This book can be used as a personal or team effort. Studying alone is always good, but when you have a partner there is always someone to hold you accountable and learn with you. Take this book on as a personal challenge to continue educating yourself since school is over with.

If you are an audio learner, you can get an audio version of this book to listen to on the way to and from work. If you are a visual learner, this book may be enough. Lastly, if you are a kinesthetic learner we have different practices available to you on our site. There you can have access to worksheets, study guides and other tools for learning. All available at www.wordsevery.com.

So however you decide to soak in these words and make them a natural part of your vocabulary, we are here to help you one word at a time.

Words Every Professional Should Know

# General Professionals

This section is for anyone who is a working professional, and/or simply wants to improve his or her vocabulary to sound more professional and distinguished. All of the words in the general professionals section can be used in any environment and in all forms of communications. You will find better synonyms for ordinary words that are used on a daily basis and words that can more distinctively describe exactly what you want to say.


**Abrogate** [ab-ruh-geyt]  Verb
To abolish, or do away with by formal or official means.
*Slavery was abrogated by Abraham Lincoln.*

**Accede** [ak-seed] Verb
To agree, give consent or adhere.
*I acceded to the terms of the contract.*

**Acquiesce** [ak-wee-es] Verb
To submit or comply silently, or without protest.
*Tom usually acquiesces halfheartedly in our business decisions.*

**Acumen** [*uh*-kyoo-m*uh*] Noun
The ability to make good judgments and quick decisions, typically in a particular domain.
*It is great to have business acumen within the business world.*

**Ambiguity** [am-bi-gyoo-i-tee] Noun
Doubtfulness or uncertainty as regards interpretation.
*In controversial situations I am plagued with moral ambiguity.*

**Ameliorate** [*uh*-meel-y*uh*-reyt] Verb
To make or become better, or more satisfactory.
*Create strategies to ameliorate negative effects on the environment.*

**Analogy** [*uh*-nal-*uh*-jee] Noun
A simliarity between like features of two things on which a comparison may be based.
*I see no analogy between your problem and mine.*

**Antithesis** [an-tith-*uh*-sis] Noun
The direct opposite; Contrast.
*Her behavior was the very antithesis of cowardly.*

**Arbitrate** [ahr-bi-treyt] Verb
(Of an independent person or body) reach an authoritative judgement or settlement.
*The board has the power to arbitrate in disputes.*

**Arcane** [ahr-keyn] Adjective
Understood by few; mysterious or secret.
*A theory filled with arcane details.*

**Articulate** [ahr-tik-y*uh*-lit; ahr-tik-y*uh*-leyt] Adj.,Verb
Uttered clearly in distinct syllables. Adj.
*I articulate my words so that everyone can understand what I am saying.*
To give clarity or distinction to. V.
*I am attempting to articulate how exactly how this painting makes me feel.*

**Assiduous** [*uh*-sij-oo-*uh*s] Adjective
Constant; working diligently at a task.
*I train assiduously for the Olympics.*

**Atrocious** [*uh*-troh-sh*uh*s] Adjective
Shockingly bad or tasteless; dreadful;
*That atrocious painting can't go up on the wall.*

**Benchmarking** [bench-mahrk] Noun
Any standard or reference by which others can be measured or judged.
*The current price for crude oil may become the benchmark.*

**Besiege** [bih-seej] Verb
To crowd around; crowd in upon; surround.
*Vacationers besieged the travel office.*

**Blunder** [bluhn-der] Noun
A gross, stupid, or careless mistake.
*That's your second blunder this morning.*

**Cachinnate** [kak-*uh*-neyt] Noun
To laugh loudly or immoderately.
*When watching comedy shows, I cachinnate the entire time.*

**Carpe diem** [kahr-pee dahy-uh m] Latin
Seize the day; enjoy the present, as opposed to placing all hope in the future.
*When I am stressed about the future, my granny always says "carpe diem."*

**Cede** [seed] Verb
To yield or formally; surrender to another.
*When a war is lost, that country must cede territory.*

**Circumspect** [sur-k*uh* m-spekt] Adjective
Watchful discreet; cautious; prudent.
*The detective must exhibit circumspect behavior.*

**Clandestine**[klan-des-tin] adjective
Characterized by, done in, or executed with secrecy or concealment, especially for purposes of supervision or deception.
*Their clandestine meetings went undiscovered for two years.*

**Cognition** [kog-nish-*uh* n] Noun
The act or process of knowing; perception.
*They exist for us only in our cognition of them.*

Words Every Professional Should Know

**Collaborate** [kuh-lab-uh-reyt] Verb
Work jointly on an activity, especially to produce or create something.
*"He collaborated with a distinguished painter on the designs"*

**Collegial** [kuh-lee-gee-uh l] Adjective
Of or characterized by the collective responsibility shared by each of a group of colleagues.
*We had a collegial conversation in the last snowfall of the season.*

**Colloquial** [k*uh*-loh-kwee-*uh* l] Adjective
Characteristic of or appropriate to ordinary or familiar conversation rather than formal speech or writing.
*My speeches are usually colloquial, so that everyone can relate.*

**Contrive** [kuh n-trahyv] Verb
To bring about or effect by a plan or scheme; manage.
*He contrived to gain their votes.*

**Conundrum** [kuh-nuhn-druh m] Noun
A riddle, the answer to which involves a pun or play on words.
*My favorite conundrum is "what is black and white and read all over? A newspaper.*

**Correlation** [kor-uh-ley-shuh n] Noun
Mutual relation of two or more things or parts.
*Studies find a positive correlation between severity of illness and nutritional status of the patients.*

**Cumulative** [kyoo-myuh-luh-tiv] Adjective
Increasing or growing by accumulation or successive additions.
*The cumulative effect of one rejection after another.*

**Decorum** [dih- kohr -uh m] Noun
Dignified propriety of behavior, speech or dress.
*You should always maintain a certain level of decorum at work.*

**Decree** [dih-kree] Noun
A formal and authoritative order, especially one having the force of law.
*A presidential decree.*

**Desultory** [des-*uh* l-tohr-ee] Adjective
Lacking in consistency, constancy, or visible order.
*I don't understand when we have desultory conversations.*

**Disconcert** [dis-kuh n-surt] Verb
To disturb the self-possession of; perturb; ruffle.
Her angry reply disconcerted *me completely.*

**E.g.** Latin
For example; for the sake of example; such as.
*There are some things for which the Salahis cannot be forgiven: e.g. canceling their appearance on Larry King Live.*

Words Every Professional Should Know

### Eclectic [ih-klek-tik] Adjective
Made up of what is selected from different sources.
*An eclectic mix of idealistic and opportunistic politicians and NGOs mobilized people against land acquisitions.*

### Eloquence [el-uh-kwuh ns] Noun
The practice or art of using language with fluency and aptness.
*It is no wonder that these words about waging peace perished his eloquence about waging war.*

### Emergent [ih-mur-juh nt] Adjective
Coming into view or notice.
*Emergent technologies have fed new and darkly ravenous appetites.*

### Enigma [*uh*-nig-m*uh*] Noun
A puzzling or inexplicable occurrence or situation.
*His disappearance is an enigma that has given rise too much speculation.*

### Epitome [ih-pit-uh-mee] Noun
A person or thing that is typical of or possesses to a high degree the features of a whole class.
*He is the epitome of goodness.*

### Erudite [er-y*oo*-dahyt] Adjective
Characterized by great knowledge; learned or scholarly.
*An erudite professor can teach you many things.*

**Euphemism** [yoo-fuh-miz-uh m] Noun
The substitution of a mild, indirect, or vague expression for one thought to be offensive, harsh, or blunt.
*The euphemism of losing "situational awareness" could be an evasive way of describing just this altered state.*

**Exasperate** [ig-zas-puh-reyt] Verb
To irritate or provoke to a high degree; extremely annoy.
*He was exasperated by the senseless delays.*

**Existential** [eg-zi-sten-shuh l] Adjective
Pertaining to existence.
*The world of sports is having something of an existential crisis, or at least it should be.*

**Exponential** [ek-spoh-nen-shuh l, -spuh-] Adjective
Having one or more unknown variables in one or more exponents.
*Yet the exponential decline in the cost means that the threat posed by the fabrication of lethal bio pathogens is rising.*

**Facile** [fas-il] Adjective
Moving, acting or working with ease.
*A facile mind is a terrible thing to waste.*

**Fidus Achates** [fīdəs əkädēz] Latin Noun
A faithful friend or companion.
*Imani is my Fidus Achates time after time.*

**Formative** [fawr-muh-tiv] Adjective
Giving form or shape; molding:
*Packaging is a formative process in manufacturing.*

**Henceforth** [hens-fawrth] Adverb
From now on; from this point forward.
*Henceforth, the media will have no clue as to what the jury might be focusing upon.*

**Hyperbole** [hahy-pur-buh-lee] Noun
Obvious and intentional exaggeration. Figure of speech not intended to be taken literally.
*Waiting an eternity is my favorite hyperbole.*

**I.e.** Latin
That is.
*You must be an amateur, i.e. someone who has never competed for prize money in athletics.*

**Impertinent** [im-pur-tn-uh nt] Adjective
Not showing proper respect; rude.
*Asking an elderly person their age can be an impertinent question.*

**Impetus** [im-pi-tuh s] Noun
A moving force; impulse; stimulus.
*The grant for building the opera house gave impetus to the city's cultural life.*

**Incongruous** [in-kong-groo-uh s] Adjective
Out of keeping or place; inappropriate; unbecoming.
*Sex in public is an incongruous behavior.*

**Indubitable** [in-doo-bi-tuh-buh l,]
That cannot be doubted; patently evident or certain.
*After seeing his face, it is indubitable that he is the father of that child.*

**Infallible** [in-fal-uh-buh l] Adjective
Absolutely trustworthy or sure:
Drinking tea is *an infallible remedy for stress.*

**Jargon** [jahr-g*uh* n] Noun
The language, especially the vocabulary, to a particular profession or group.
*Manifesting things from out of nowhere is holistic healing jargon.*

**Jocular** [jok-yuh-ler] Adjective
Given to, characterized by, intended for joking or jesting.
Jocular remarks about *opera stars.*

**Juxtaposition** [juhk-st*uh*-p*uh*-zish-*uh* n] Noun
An act or instance of placing close together or side by side, especially for comparison or contrast.
*The juxtaposition of "luxury yachts" and "wind turbines" is especially cute.*

**Lexicon** [lek-si-kon, -k*uh* n] Noun
The vocabulary of a particular language, field or people.
*If "umami" was recently accepted into the lexicon, then maybe "tomato-ey" isn't that far behind.*

**Loath** [loh*th*] Adjective
Unwilling; reluctant; disinclined; averse.
*To be loath to admit a mistake.*

**Loathe** [loh*th*] Verb
To feel disgust or intense aversion for.
*I loathe people who spread malicious gossip.*

**Malice** [mal-is] Noun
Desire to inflict injury, harm, or suffering on another, either because of a hostile impulse or out of deep-seated meanness.
*The malice and spite of a lifelong enemy.*

**Nominal** [nom-*uh*-nl] Adjective
Being such in name only; so-called; putative.
*A man is the nominal head of the household.*

**Odium** [oh-dee-uh m] Noun
Intense hatred or dislike, especially toward a person or thing regarded as contemptible, despicable or repugnant.
*I have a real odium for bad smells.*

**Ostentatious** [os-ten-tey-shuh s, -tuh n-] Adjective
Characterized by or given to pretentious or conspicuous show in an attempt to impress others:
*An ostentatious dresser is always looking good in public.*

### Oxymoron [ok-si- mohr -on]
A figure of speech by which a locution produces an incongruous, seemingly self-contradictory effect.
*He is so gorgeously ugly, is a great oxymoron to describe her.*

### Pandemic [pan-dem-ik] Adjetcive
(Of a disease) prevalent throughout an entire country, continent or the whole world; epidemic over a large area.
*Malaria has been a pandemic to many places.*

### Paradox [par-uh-doks] Noun
A statement or proposition that seems self-contradictory or absurd but in reality expresses a possible truth.
*As I was listening to these remarks, I kept thinking to myself about this paradox.*

### Paraphernalia [par-uh-fer-neyl-yuh] Noun
Equipment, apparatus, or furnishing used in or necessary for a particular activity.

*A skier's paraphernalia is necessary for safety.*

### Paraphrase [par-uh-freyz] Noun
A restatement of a text or passage giving the meaning in another form, as for clearness; rewording.
*To paraphrase Hemingway, climate change first comes gradually then all at once.*

### Patrician [puh-trish-uh n] Noun
A person of noble or high rank; aristocrat.
*President Obama is the No.1 Patrician of the U.S..*

### Piquant [pee-kuh nt] Adjective
Agreeably pungent or sharp in taste or flavor; pleasant biting or tart.
*A piquant jelly is the best for a memorable tasting sandwich.*

### Recourse [ree-kohrs] Noun
Access or resort to a person or thing for help or protection.
*To have recourse to the courts for justice.*

### Retort [ri-tawrt] verb
To reply to, usually in a sharp or retaliatory way.
*It was a few seconds before I managed a retort: "Whatever."*

### Rhetoric [ret-er-ik] Noun
(In writing or speech) the undue use of exaggeration or display.
*How extreme does a candidate need to sound in his or her tone and rhetoric to satisfy them?*

### Sojourn [soh-jurn] Noun
A temporary stay.
*He met sue during his sojourn in Paris.*

### Soliloquy [suh-lil-uh-kwee] Noun
An utterance or discourse by a person who is talking to himself or herself or is disregardful of or obvious to any hearers present.
*Hamlet's soliloquy begins with "To be or not to be."*

**Sublime** [suh-blahym] Adjective
Elevated or lofty in thought or language.
*Paradise Lost is sublime poetry.*

**Superfluous** [soo-pur-floo-uh s] Adjective
Being more than is sufficient or required; excessive.
*The device of reconstructing internal dialogues sometimes feels a bit forced or superfluous.*

**Syntax** [sin-taks] Noun
Linguistics.
*Butler's syntax sometimes gets in the way of understanding what she's asserting as fact.*

**Toil** [toil] Noun
Hard and continuous work; exhausting labor or effort.
*But football is a game in which a moment of magic can undo an hour of toil.*

**Transcendent** [tran-sen-duh nt] Adjective
Going beyond ordinary limits; surpassing; exceeding.
*It's seen as behaving dreadfully or behaving with transcendent virtue.*

**Ubiquitous** [yoo-bik-wi-tuh s] Adjective
Existing or being everywhere, especially at the same time.
*On a dark scary night there is ubiquitous fog.*

**Unilateral** [yoo-nuh-lat-er-uh l] Adjective
Relating to, occurring on, or involving one side only.
Unilateral development typically fixes the better side of town.

**Vernacular** [ver-nak-yuh-ler] Adjective
(Of language) native or indigenous (opposed to literary or learned).
*It was amusing, it was in my vernacular, and the atmosphere held great emotional resonance for me.*

Words Every Professional Should Know

# **Business**

These words are for more refined business environments. In business there are certain keywords that are used in order to maintain a consistent level of prestige and distinction. Whether you are conversing with colleagues or drafting an email to your CEO, these words can assist with a more polished approach.

**Accordance** [*uh*-kawr-dns] Noun
Agreement; conformity.
*In accordance with the rules.*

**Acquisition** [ak-wuh-zish-uh n] Noun
The act of acquiring or gaining possession.
*The acquisition of real estate.*

**Aforementioned** [uh-fawr-men-shuh nd] Adjective
Cited or mentioned earlier or previously.
*Besides the aforementioned, these are all great things.*

## Words Every Professional Should Know

**Anodyne** [an-uh-dahyn] Noun
Anything that relieves distress or pain.
*The music was an anodyne to his grief.*

**Aplomb** [uh-plom] Noun
Imperturbable self-possession, poise, or assurance.
*When he needed to put Rick Perry and Rick Santorum away during the primaries, by God he did it, and with aplomb.*

**Arcane** [ahr-keyn] Adjective
Known or understood by very few; mysterious; secret.
*She knew a lot about Sanskrit grammar and other arcane matters.*

**Ardent** [ahr-dnt] Adjective
Having, expressive of, or characterized by intense feeling; passionate.
*When getting married, an ardent vow is made.*

**Arrogate** [ar-uh geyt] Verb
To claim presumptuously; assume or appropriate to oneself without right.
*To arrogate the right to make decisions.*

**Bandwidth** [band-width, -with]
Telecommunications. The smallest range of frequencies constituting a band within which a particular signal can be transmitted without distortion.
*Users also require the bandwidth and patience to download large files.*

**Bureaucracy** [by*oo*-**rok**-r*uh*-see] Noun
Government by many bureaus, administrators, and petty officials.
*In other words, what was once a matter of law, however imperfect, is now a matter of bureaucracy.*

**Candor** [kan-der] Noun
The state or quality of being frank, open and sincere in speech or expression; candidness.
*The candor of the speech impressed the audience.*

**Collegiality** [kuh-lee-jee-al-i-tee, -gee-] Noun
Cooperative interaction among colleagues.
*Wyden is popular with GOP colleagues for his collegiality, work ethic and willingness to include their ideas in legislation.*

**Cumulative** [kyoo-myuh-luh-tiv] Adjective
Increasing or growing by accumulation or successive additions.
*The cumulative effect of one rejection after another.*

**Dexterity** [dek-ster-i-tee] Noun
Skill using the hands or body; agility.
*It was a reminder that regardless of how outrageous the setting may be, one cannot deny Browne's dexterity in designing clothes.*

**Diligent** [dil-i-juh nt] Adjective
Constant in effort to accomplish something; attentive and persistent in doing anything.
*A diligent student is likely to get an A in a class.*

**Fabricate** [fab-ri-keyt] Verb
To make by art or skill and labor; construct.
*The finest craftspeople fabricated this clock.*

**Inadequate** [in-ad-i-kwit] Adjective
Not adequate or sufficient.
*He is inadequate because he does not have the proper training.*

**Incentivize** [in-sen-ti-vahyz] Verb
To give incentives to.
*The government should allow incentives in order to create jobs.*

**Incisive** [in-sahy-siv] Adjective
Penetrating; cutting; biting.
*An incisive tone of voice.*

**Inept** [in-ept] Adjective
Without skill or aptitude for a particular task or assignment.
*He is inept at mechanical tasks.*

**Jocular** [jok-yuh-ler] Adjective
Given to, characterized by, intended for, or suited to joking or jesting.
*Jocular remarks about operators.*

## Words Every Professional Should Know

**Leaflet** [leef-lit] Noun
A small flat or folded sheet of printed matter, as an advertisement or notice, usually intended for free intended for free distribution.
*Bogucki includes the leaflet in a PowerPoint presentation he has developed.*

**Monetization** [mon-i-tahyz, muhn-] Verb
To legalize money.
*This green paper has to go through monetization in order to become actual dividends.*

**Notoriety** [noh-tuh-rahy-i-tee] Noun
The state, quality or character of being notorious or widely known.
*A craze for notoriety can come off narcissistic.*

**Nugatory** [noo-guh-tawr-ee] Adjective
Of no real value; trifling; worthless.
*Therefore all art which involves no reference to man is inferior or nugatory.*

**Paradigm** [par-uh-dahym] Noun
A typical example or pattern of something; a model.
*"There is a new paradigm for public art in this country."*

**Parvenu** [pahr-vuh-noo] Noun
A person of obscure origin who has gained wealth, influence, or celebrity.
*"The political inexperience of a parvenu."*

**Perfunctory** [per-fuhngk-tuh-ree] Adjective
Performed merely as a routine duty; hasty and superficial.
*Thank you should be a perfunctory courtesy.*

**Polymath** [pol-ee-math] Noun
A person of great learning in several fields of study.
*She is the perfect candidate for jeopardy because she is a polymath.*

**Preferential** [pref-uh-ren-shuh l] Adjective
Showing or giving preference.
*A preferential hiring system.*

**Punctilio** [puhngk-til-ee-oh] Noun
A fine point, particular, or detail, as of conduct, ceremony, or procedure.
*This punctilio is best for singing happy birthday.*

**Quintessential** [kwin-tuh-sen-shuh l] Adjective
Of the pure and essential essence of something.
*The quintessential Jewish delicatessen.*

**Regnant** [reg-nuh nt] Adjective
Reigning; ruling.
*It is difficult to assert a timid individuality in the presence of a regnant force.*

**Residual** [ri-zij-oo-uh l] Adjective
Pertaining to or constituting a residue remainder; remaining; leftover.
*There is a lot of residual concern that Lizard Squad was able to get even this far.*

**Seriatim** [seer-ee-ey-tim, ser-] Adverb
In a series; one after another.
*All right" I said "we shall take them in proper season and deal with them seriatim.*

**Severance** [sev-er-uh ns] Noun
The action of ending a connection or relationship.
*"The severance and disestablishment of the Irish Church."*

**Sinecure** [sahy-ni-kyoo r, sin-i-] Noun
An office or position requiring little or no work, especially one yielding profitable returns.
*The job is often a sinecure offered to widely admired figures.*

**Sobriquet** [soh-bruh-key] Noun
A nickname.
*There is a report that some of his political foes, playing upon his initials, saddle him with the sobriquet of "rat."*

**Spurious** [spyoo r-ee-uh s] Adjective
Not genuine, authentic, or true; pretended; counterfeit.
*Corry argues that this is merely a political opinion, backed by questionable and spurious data.*

**Sustainability** [suh-stey-nuh-bil-i-tee] Noun
The ability to be sustained, supported, upheld or confirmed.
*Of course, as is often the case, there is a price to be paid for sustainability.*

**Synergy** [sin-er-jee] Noun
The interaction or cooperation of two or more organizations, substances, or other agents to produce a combined effect greater than the sum of their separate effects.
*"The synergy between artist and record company"*

**Tenacity** [tuh-nas-i-tee] Noun
The quality of being tenacious, or of holding fast; persistence.
*The amazing tenacity of rumors.*

**Unison** [yoo-nuh-suh n] Noun
Simultaneous performance of action or utterance of speech.
*"Yes, sir," said the girls in unison.*

**Velocity** [vuh-los-i-tee] Noun
Rapidity of motion or operation; swiftness; speed.
*A high wind velocity.*

**Venal** [veen-l] Adjective
Willing to sell one's influence, especially in return especially in return for a bribe; open to bribery; mercenary.
*A venal judge is willing to accept things for money.*

**Voracity** [Voh-ras-i-tee] Noun
The condition of being eager to consume a great amount of food, or marked by an insatiable appetite.
*Only Rangoon vultures surpassed them in numbers and voracity.*

**Zeal** [zeel] Noun
Fervor for a person, cause, or object; eager desire or endeavor; enthusiastic diligence.
*One of those preachers admitted to The Daily Beast that he was taken aback by her zeal.*

# Words Every Professional Should Know

# Communications

Good oral and written communication is the one thing everyone expects you to have. While holding conversations or giving a speech there are certain words that can assist with describing things and creating a tone within your delivery. Whether in the communications field, or not, this section is great for all that use communications on a daily basis; which is everyone.

**Affiliate** [*uh*-fil-ee-eyt] Verb
To bring into close association or connection.
*The research center is affiliated with the university.*

**Aggregate** [ag-ri-git] Adjective
Formed by the conjunction or collection of particulars collection of particulars into a whole mass or sum; total; combined.
*The aggregate amount of indebtedness.*

**Aphorism** [af-uh-riz-uh m] Noun
A pithy observation that contains a general truth.
*My favorite aphorism is "if it ain't broke, don't fix it."*

**Bespeak** [bih-speek] Verb
To ask for in advance.
*To bespeak the reader's patience.*

**Burgeon** [bur-juh n] Verb
To grow or develop quickly; flourish.
*The town burgeoned into a city.*

**Calumny** [kal-uh m-nee] Noun
A false and malicious statement designed to injure the reputation of someone or something.
*The speech was considered a calumny of the administration.*

**Commerce** [kom-ers] Noun
An interchange of goods or commodities, especially on a large scale between different countries (foreign commerce) or between parts of the same country (domestic commerce) trade; business.
*Since the powerful Arizona Chamber of commerce oppose the measure Brewer likely will veto it.*

**Compulsory** [kuh m-puhl-suh-ree] Adjective
Required; mandatory; obligatory.
*Foreign language is a compulsory prerequisite for college.*

### Consensus [kuh n-sen-suh s] Noun
Majority of opinion.
*The consensus of the group was that they should meet twice a month.*

### Content [kon-tent] Noun
Usually, contents.
- Something that is contained:
- The contents of a box.
- The subjects or topics covered in a book or document.
- The chapters or other formal divisions of a book or document:

*A table of contents.*

### Curtail [ker-teyl] Verb
Reduce in extent or quantity; impose a restriction on.
*"Civil liberties were further curtailed."*

### Decorum [dih-kawr-uh m, -kohr-] Noun
Behavior in keeping with good taste and propriety.
*"You exhibit remarkable modesty and decorum."*

### Emporium [em-pawr-ee-uh m] Noun
A large retail store, especially one selling a great variety of articles.
*I go to the emporium anytime I need anything.*

### Enquiry [en-kwahyuh r-ee] Noun
An act of asking for information.
*"The deluge of phone enquiry after a crash."*

**Exploit** [ek-sploit, ik-sploit] Noun
A striking or notable deed; feat; spirited or heroic act.
*The exploits of Alexander the Great.*

**Felicity** [fi-lis-i-tee] Noun
The state of being happy, especially in a high degree; bliss.
*Marital felicity means you married the right person.*

**Futile** [fyoot-l, fyoo-tahyl] Adjective
Incapable of producing any result; ineffective; useless; not successful.
*Attempting to force-feed the sick horse was futile.*

**Hospitable** [hos-pi-tuh-buh l] Adjective
Receiving or treating guests or strangers warmly and generously.
*A hospitable family always makes you feel good in their home.*

**Illocutionary** [il-uh-kyoo-shuh-ner-ee] Adjective
Pertaining to a linguistic act performed by a speaker in producing an utterance, as suggesting, warning, promising, or requesting.
*"I pronounce you man and wife" is a descriptive statement, but also has illocutionary force.*

**Manqué** [mahng-key] Adjective
Having failed, missed, or fallen short, especially because of circumstances or a defect of character; unsuccessful.
*A poet manqué who never produced a single book of verse.*

**Mendacious** [men-dey-shuh s] Adjective
Telling lies, especially habitually; dishonest; lying; untruthful.
*A mendacious person is very untrustworthy.*

**Netiquette** [net-i-kit, ket] Noun
The rules of etiquette that apply when communicating over computer networks, especially the internet.
*Kern had risen with her, though she had not learned that from the netiquette.*

**Paralinguistic** [par-uh-ling-gwis-tik] Adjective
Of, relating to, or denoting paralanguage or the no lexical elements of communication by speech.
*The conversational use of spoken language cannot be properly understood unless paralinguistic elements are take into account."*

**Perdition** [per-dish-uh n] Noun
A state of final spiritual ruin; loss of the soul; damnation.
*Sinners condemned to eternal perdition.*

**Philistine** [fil-uh-steen] Noun
A person who is lacking in or hostile or smugly indifferent to cultural values, intellectual pursuits, aesthetic refinement, etc., or is contentedly commonplace in ideas and tastes.
*He is one in revolt with Byron and Shelley against a philistine world.*

**Sanguine** [sang-gwin] Adjective
Cheerfully optimistic, hopeful, or confident.
*If you always have sanguine expectations some things may feel inevitable.*

### SEO – search engine optimization
The methods used to boost the ranking or frequency of a website in results returned by a search engine in an effort to maximize user traffic to the site.
*The first step in SEO is to generate keywords that are relevant to your site's content.*

**Solecism** [sol-uh-siz-uh m] Noun
A breach of good manners or etiquette.
*He committed solecism when he decided to flash everyone.*

**Veracity** [vuh-ras-i-tee] Noun
Habitual observance of truth in speech or statement; truthfulness.
*He was not noted for his veracity.*

# Finance

Within the financial industry there are words that are specialized to be used to describing numbers and financial situations. This section will increase your terminology for dealing with dividends, taxes and corporate financial and accounting situations.

**Consolidate** [k*uh* n-sol-i-deyt] Verb
To bring together (separate parts) into a single or unified whole; unite; combine.
*I consolidated my June and July bills in order to pay at once.*

**Deficit** [def-uh-sit] Noun.
The amount by which a sum of money falls short of the required amount.
*And the weak economic recovery makes this hard task even harder in other deficit countries like the U.K.*

**Defray** [dih-frey] Verb
To bear or pay all or part of (the costs, expenses, etc.)
*The grant helped defray the expenses of the trip.*

**Deplete** [dih-pleet] Noun
To decrease seriously or exhaust the abundance or supply of.
*I depleted my savings account after that vacation.*

**Efficient** [ih-fish-uh nt] Adjective
Performing or functioning in the best possible manner with the least waste of time and; having and using requisite knowledge, skill and industry; competent;
*I manage my crew to be more efficient everyday.*

**Embezzle** [em-bez-uh l] Verb
To appropriate fraudulently to one's own use, as money or property entrusted to one's care.
*The governor embezzled 2.1 million dollars from local accounts.*

**Exorbitant** [ig-zawr-bi-tuh nt] Adjective
Exceeding the bounds of custom, propriety, or reason, especially in amount or extent; highly excessive.
*To charge an exorbitant price.*

**Feasible** [fee-zuh-buh l] Adjective
Capable of being done, effected, or accomplished.
This I a feasible plan to escape from debt.

**Forbearance** [fawr-bair-uh ns] Noun
A creditor's giving of indulgence after the day originally fixed for payment.
*My loan went into forbearance after the 1st.*

### Formulate [fawr-myuh-leyt] Verb
To express in precise form; state definitely or systematically.
*He finds it extremely difficult to formulate his new theory.*

### Fractional [frak-shuh-nl] Adjective
Pertaining to fractions; comprising a part or the parts of a unit; constituting a fraction.
*The profit on the deal was fractional.*

### Illicit [ih-lis-it] Adjective
Not legally permitted or authorized; unlicensed; unlawful.
*I don't think it's inherently tragic when a mother of three young adults goes chasing after some illicit euphoria.*

### Judicious [joo-dish-uh s] Adjective
Using or showing judgment as to action or practical expediency; discreet, prudent or politic.
*Judicious use of one's money.*

### Lucrative [loo-kruh-tiv] Adjective
Profitable; moneymaking.
*Investing in stocks can be a lucrative venture.*

### Magnate [mag-neyt, -nit] Noun
A person of great influence, importance, or standing in particular enterprise, field of business.
*You should always trust the railroad magnate.*

**Marginally** [mahr-juh-nl] Adverb
Selling goods at a price that just equals the additional cost of producing the last unit supplied.
*Arkansas had been marginally healthier than the states surrounding it.*

**Monetize** [mon-i-tahyz, muhn-] Verb
To legalize as money.
*I have to monetize this green paper to be worth something.*

**Notional** [noh-shuh-nl] Adjective
Pertaining to or expressing a notion or idea.
*A notional response to the question.*

**Nullify** [nuhl-uh-fahy] Verb
To render or declare legally void or inoperative.
*After nonpayment, the contract was nullified.*

**Par** [pahr] Noun
An equality in value or standing; a level of equality.
*The gains and the losses are on a par.*

**Peripheral** [puh-rif-er-uh l] Adjective
Pertaining to, situated in, or constituting the periphery.
*Peripheral resistance on the outskirts of the battle area.*

**Pilfer** [pil-fer] Verb
To steal, especially in small quantities.
*The women and children beg and pilfer, and the men commit greater acts of dishonesty.*

**Solvency** [sol-vuh n-see] Noun
Ability to pay all just debts.
*In the past months, those fears–combined with real concerns about the solvency of Italy– have been intensifying.*

# Words Every Professional Should Know

Words Every Professional Should Know

# Health & Wellness

The lingo here is best used for explaining and describing situations and conditions that are more prevalent within the medical industry. This also includes other forms of wellness, specifically energy healing practices.

**Atonement** [*uh*-tohn-m*uh* nt] Noun
Reparation for a wrong or injury.
*She wanted to make atonement for her husband's behavior.*

**Catabolism** [kuh-tab-uh-liz-uh m] Noun
Destructive metabolism; the breaking down in living ones, with the release of energy.
*Hering has long insisted on a self-regulative adjustment of the cell metabolism, so that action involves reaction, increased catabolism necessitates after-increase of anabolism.*

**Debility** [dih-bil-i-tee] Noun
A weakened or enfeebled state; weakness.
*Debility prevented him from getting out of bed.*

### Deficiency [dih-fish-uh n-see] Noun
The state of being deficient; lack; incompleteness; insufficiency.
*It is the deficiency, and not the excess of this quality, that is to be feared.*

### Disintegrate [dis-in-tuh-greyt] Verb
Break up into small parts, typically as the result of impact or decay.
*When the missile struck, the car disintegrated in a sheet of searing flame.*

### Duress [doo-res] Noun
Compulsion by threat or force; coercion; constraint.
*Confessions extracted under duress.*

### Enervation [en-er-veyt] Verb
A feeling of being drained of energy or vitality; fatigue.
*A sense of enervation.*

### Eudemonia [yoo-di-moh-nee-uh] Noun
Happiness; well-being.
*I always flourish in eudemonia situations with friends and family.*

### Eustress [yoo-stres] Noun
Stress that is deemed healthful or giving one the feeling.
*Anytime my job causes eustress, I am happy to return the next day.*

## Words Every Professional Should Know

**Evade** [ih-veyd] Verb
To escape from by trickery or cleverness.
*To evade one's pursuers.*

**Feebleness** [fee-buh l] Adjective
Physically weak, as from age or sickness; frail.
*Once she started treatment, we noticed her feebleness stature.*

**Grievance** [gree-vuh ns] Noun
A wrong considered as grounds for complaint, or something believed to cause distress.
*Inequitable taxation is the chief grievance.*

**Holistic** [hoh-lis-tik] Adjective
Incorporating the concept of holism, or the idea that the whole is more than merely the sum of its parts, in theory or practice.
*Holistic psychology encompasses more aspects that one.*

**Immunization** [im-yuh-nuh-zey-shuh n] Noun
The fact or process of becoming immune, as against a disease.
*This shot will give me the immunization I need against malaria.*

**Languor** [lang-ger] Noun
Lack of energy or vitality; sluggishness.
*He suddenly saw Tom stir, and he came from his state of languor.*

**Manifest** [man-uh-fest] Adjective
Psychoanalysis. Of or relating to conscious feelings, ideas, and impulses that contain repressed psychic material.
*The manifest content of a dream as opposed to the latent content that it conceals.*

**Metabolic** [met-uh-bol-ik] Adjective
Of, relating to, or affected by metabolism.
*Dangerously low calorie intake and a high risk of metabolic shock.*

**Olfactory** [ol-fak-tuh-ree] Adjective
Of or relating to the sense of smell.
*Olfactory organs are usually found in dead animals.*

**Regimen** [rej-uh-muh n] Noun
A prescribed course of medical treatment, way of life, or diet for the promotion or restoration of health.
*A regimen of one or two injections per day.*

**Reiki** [rei-ki] Noun
A healing technique based on the principle that the therapist can channel energy into the patient by means of touch, to activate the natural healing processes of the patient's body and restore physical and emotional well-being.
*He gave me trike while I was going through my divorce to make me feel better.*

**Senility** [si-nil-i-tee] Noun
The state of being senile, especially the weakness or mental infirmity of old age.
*While experiencing senility she ran across the street toward oncoming traffic.*

**Vigorous** [vig-er-uh s] Adjective
Strong; active; robust.
*He is such a vigorous youngster.*

# Words Every Professional Should Know

# Supply Chain & Transportation

The transportation industry uses terms to describe vehicles, sizes, ranges, materials and many others. These words can assist with specialized terminology and provide more descriptive words for those within the industry.

**Altitudinous** [al-ti-tood -n-*uh* s] Adjective
Extending to a great distance upward, lofty, indefinitely high.
*It's situated atop an altitudinous building.*

**Append** [uh-pend] Verb
To add as a supplement, accessory, or appendix.
*Please append that trailer to this truck for me.*

**Compliance** [kuh m-plahy-uh ns] Noun
The act of conforming, acquiescing, or yielding.
*Every doctor must be in compliance with state regulations.*

**Convene** [kuh n-veen] Verb
To come together or assemble, usually for some public purpose.
*We will convene at noon tomorrow.*

**Defunct** [dih-fuhngkt] Adjective
No longer in effect or use; not operating or functioning.
*A defunct law; a defunct organization.*

**Docket** [dok-it] Noun
The list of business to be transacted by a board, council, legislative assembly, or the like.
*Reevaluating is on the docket for tonight's meeting.*

**Erode** [ih-rohd] Verb
To eat into or away; destroy by slow consumption or disintegration.
*Battery acid had eroded the engine. Inflation erodes the value of our money.*

**Fickle** [fik-uh l] Adjective
Likely to change, especially due to caprice, irresolution, or instability; casually changeable.
*In the spring the weather is very fickle.*

**Freight** [freyt] Noun
Goods, cargo, or lading transported for pay, whether by water, land, or air.
*Wal-Mart had contracted T&T to transport their freight.*

### Gauge [geyj] Verb
Any device or instrument for measuring, registering measurements, or testing something, especially for measuring a dimension, quantity, or mechanical accuracy.
*I used the pressure gauge to check my tires.*

### Hauler [haw-ler] Noun
A person, commercial trucking company or vehicle that is designed for hauling things.
*I needed a 20,000 lb hauler for the mobile home transport job.*

### Hone [hohn] Noun
A whetstone of fine, compact texture for sharpening razors and other cutting tools.
*I used the hone for my fishing knife.*

### Inadmissible [in-uh d-mis-uh-buh l] Adjective
Not admissible; not allowable.
*Such evidence would be inadmissible in any court.*

### Inertia [in-ur-shuh] Noun
Inertness, especially with regard to effort, motion, action, and the like; inactivity; sluggishness.
*Inertia sometimes keeps us from breaking free and what we know in our minds that we should do.*

### Inoperative [in-op-er-uh-tiv] Adjective
Not operative; not in operation.
*The train that was in an accident is inoperative.*

### Jettison [jet-uh-suh n] Verb
To cast (goods) overboard in order to lighten a vessel or aircraft or to improve its stability in an emergency.
*LaFever had almost made it to the lake, but slowly had to jettison all of his gear, as he got weaker.*

### Languish [lang-gwish] Verb
To be or become weak or feeble; droop; fade.
*They see people just like them being elevated quickly to power while they languish, and they become envious.*

### Latent [leyt-nt] Adjective
Present but not visible, apparent, or actualized; existing as potential.
*He possessed the latent ability to move extremely heavy things.*

### Meager [mee-ger] Adjective
Deficient in quantity or quality; lacking fullness or richness; scanty; inadequate.
*I would expect to have a meager salary at the smaller company.*

### Memorandum [mem-uh-ran-duh m] Noun
A short note designating something to be remembered, especially something to be done or acted upon in the future; reminder.
*The memorandum begins by referring to the letter of "100 liberal American Jewish leaders."*

## Words Every Professional Should Know

**Moribund** [mawr-uh-buhnd] Adjective
On the verge of extinction or termination.
*Then Heal STL was burned down Monday like a moribund body for cremation.*

**Parcel** [pahr-suh l] Noun
An object, article, container, or quantity of something wrapped or packed up; small package; bundle.
*I shipped a parcel through UPS yesterday for my mother.*

**Pare** [pair] Verb
To cut off the outer coating, layer, or part of.
*After food stamp usage hit record-breaking numbers in 2013, Congress tried to pare back the benefit.*

**Plateau** [pla-toh] Noun
A land area having a relatively level surface considerably raised above adjoining land on at least one side, and often cut by deep canyons.
*You rise, you plateau, but at the end of the day everyone comes down.*

**Quasi** [kwah-see, -zee] Adjective
Resembling; seeming; virtual.
*He is only a quasi member of this board.*

**Sedentary** [sed-n-ter-ee] Adjective
Characterized by or requiring a sitting posture.
*A sedentary occupation should be easy for some people.*

Visit:

www.wordsevery.com

# References

Cambridge English Dictionary: Meanings & Definitions. (n.d.). Retrieved from http://dictionary.cambridge.org/dictionary/english

Dictionary and Thesaurus | Merriam-Webster. (n.d.). Retrieved from http://www.merriam-webster.com/

Dictionary, Encyclopedia and Thesaurus - The Free Dictionary. (n.d.). Retrieved from http://www.thefreedictionary.com/

Dictionary.com | Find the Meanings and Definitions of Words at Dictionary.com. (n.d.). Retrieved from http://dictionary.reference.com/

Oxford Dictionaries - Dictionary, Thesaurus, & Grammar. (n.d.). Retrieved from http://www.oxforddictionaries.com/

www.ingramcontent.com/pod-product-compliance
Lightning Source LLC
Chambersburg PA
CBHW061250040426
42444CB00010B/2328